# The Quotation Bank

## *The Tempest*

## William Shakespeare

Copyright © 2025 Esse Publishing Limited and Elmina Ferguson.
The moral rights of the authors have been asserted.

First published in 2024 by:
The Quotation Bank
Esse Publishing Limited

10 9 8 7 6 5 4 3 2 1

All rights reserved. No part of this publication may be reproduced, resold, stored in a retrieval system or transmitted in any form, or by any means (electronic, photocopying, mechanical or otherwise) without the prior written permission of both the copyright owners and the publisher.

A CIP catalogue record for this book is available from the British Library.
**ISBN 978-1-7396080-4-0**

All enquiries to: contact@thequotationbank.co.uk

Printed and bound by Target Print Limited, Broad Lane, Cottenham, Cambridge CB24 8SW.

www.thequotationbank.co.uk

## Introduction

| | |
|---|---|
| What examiners are looking for | 4 |
| How The Quotation Bank can help you in your exams | 5 |
| How to use The Quotation Bank | 6 |

## Quotations

| | |
|---|---|
| Act One | 7 |
| Act Two | 12 |
| Act Three | 17 |
| Act Four | 22 |
| Act Five | 27 |

## Revision and Essay Planning

| | |
|---|---|
| Major Themes and Characters | 32 |
| How to revise effectively | 33 |
| Sample essay, potential essay questions and revision activities | 34 |
| Glossary | 41 |

## Welcome to The Quotation Bank, the comprehensive guide to all the key quotations you need to succeed in your exams.

Whilst you may have read the play, watched a production, understood the plot and have a strong grasp of context, the vast majority of marks awarded in your GCSE are for the ability to write a focused essay, full of quotations, and most importantly, quotations that you then analyse.

I think we all agree it is *analysis* that is the tricky part – and that is why we are here to help!

**The Quotation Bank** takes 25 of the most important quotations from the text, interprets them, analyses them, highlights literary techniques Shakespeare has used, puts them in context, and suggests which quotations you might use in which essays.

At the end of **The Quotation Bank** we have put together a sample answer, essay plans and great revision exercises to help you prepare for your exam. We have also included a detailed glossary to make sure you completely understand what certain literary terms actually mean!

## English Literature 9-1: What are examiners looking for?

**All GCSE Exam Boards mark your exams using the same Assessment Objectives (AOs) – around 80% of your mark across the English Literature GCSE will be awarded for A01 and A02.**

| | |
|---|---|
| **A01** | Read, understand and respond to texts. Students should be able to: <br> • Maintain a critical style and develop an ***informed personal response*** <br> • Use textual references, ***including quotations***, to support and illustrate ***interpretations***. |
| **A02** | Analyse the ***Language, Form and Structure*** used by a writer to ***create meanings and effects***, using ***relevant subject terminology*** where appropriate. |

Basically, **AO1** is the ability to answer the question set, showing a good knowledge of the text, and using quotations to back up ideas and interpretations.

**AO2** is the ability to analyse these quotations, as well as the literary techniques the writer uses, and to show you understand the effect of these on the audience.

We will also highlight elements of **AO3** – the context in which the play is set.

## How The Quotation Bank can help you in your exams.

**The Quotation Bank is designed to make sure that every point you make in an essay clearly fulfils the Assessment Objectives an examiner will be using when marking your work.**

**Every quotation comes with the following detailed material:**

**Interpretation:** The interpretation of each quotation allows you to fulfil **AO1**, responding to the text and giving an informed personal response.

**Techniques:** Using subject-specific terminology correctly (in this case, the literary devices used by Shakespeare) is a key part of **AO2**.

**Analysis:** We have provided as much analysis (**AO2**) as possible. It is a great idea to analyse the quotation in detail – you need to do more than just say what it means, but also what effect the language, form and structure has on the audience.

**Use in essays on…** Your answer needs to be focused to fulfil **AO1**. This section helps you choose relevant quotations and link them together for a stronger essay.

## How to use The Quotation Bank.

Many students spend time learning quotations by heart.

This is an excellent idea, but they often forget what they are meant to do with those quotations once they get into the exam!

By using **The Quotation Bank**, not only will you have a huge number of quotations to use in your essays, you will also have ideas on what to say about them, how to analyse them, how to link them together, and what questions to use them for.

For GCSE essay questions, these quotations can form the basis of your answer, making sure every point comes **directly from the text (AO1)** and allowing you to **analyse language, form and structure (AO2)**. We also highlight where you can easily and effectively include **context (AO3)**.

For GCSE questions that give you an extract to analyse, the quotations in **The Quotation Bank** are excellent not only for revising the skills of **analysis (AO2)**, but also for showing **wider understanding of the text (AO1)**.

**Act One Scene One:**
> **SEBASTIAN:** "A pox o' your throat, you bawling, blasphemous, incharitable dog!"

**Interpretation:** The opening scene has a sense of denouncement. Antonio's fraught time with the Boatswain shows the inversion of power on the boat; whilst usually at the bottom of this immensely elitist society, the Boatswain now holds the most authority.

**Techniques:** Exclamation; Imagery; Tri-colon (or list of three); Alliteration.

**Analysis:**

- From the outset, Sebastian is presented in a negative light; his immensely supercilious manner, highlighted by dehumanising the Boatswain to no more than a "dog" and accusing him of "blasphemous" behaviour, is juxtaposed by the Boatswain's short, dismissive comments.
- Shakespeare uses visceral, combative language, hinting at the ferocious nature of the action to come. Indeed, *The Tempest* is tempestuous; the language has a fiery, volatile quality to it, reinforced by the violent associations of "bawling" and the harsh, aggressive alliteration of the 'b' sound.
- The curse of "a pox o' your throat" is rather hyperbolic; it is subtle comedy here as the terrified aristocrat loses his temper and utters unjustifiable things.

**Use in Essays on...** Violence; Power; Class.

**Act One Scene Two:**
**MIRANDA: "If by your art, my dearest father, you have / Put the wild waters in this roar, allay them."**

**Interpretation:** Miranda's opening lines echo the chaotic nature of the opening scene. In many ways, Act One Scene Two parallels Act One Scene One; the audience may see them on land, but the islanders are still caught in the tempestuous storm.

**Techniques:** Tone; Imagery.

**Analysis:**
- A character filled with contradictions, in this moment Miranda subverts the typical notion of Jacobean femininity; instead of docile, she is forthright in tone.
- Her call to "allay them" can be seen as both a plea and a demand. Read as a plea, the audience are once again presented with ideas of power and control. The audience are also made privy to the hierarchical nature of the island; whilst seemingly much less restrictive, the island still carries and mirrors the restraints of the Italian aristocracy.
- If read as a command, we are invited to examine the subtle power dynamics between Prospero and Miranda; "your art, my dearest father" is flattering in tone, yet "wild waters in this roar" could be seen as judgemental or fearful.

**Use in essays on…** Power; Gender; The Supernatural; Relationships.

**Act One Scene Two:**
> **PROSPERO:** "To what tune pleased his ear, that now he was / The ivy which had hid my princely trunk, /And sucked my verdure out on on't."

**Interpretation:** The emotion of resentment is integral to understanding Prospero's argument; he casts himself as an unwitting victim, with his brother the nefarious villain.

**Techniques:** Metaphor; Imagery; Juxtaposition.

**Analysis:**
- The use of horticultural imagery helps represent the growth of resentment, as well as the insidious way his brother stole power from him; "Ivy" is often characterised as evil due to its dominance and destruction of other plants.
- Furthermore, when considering ivy's association with the Greek god Dionysus, Prospero could be suggesting a certain element of chaos; Dionysus was characterised as being dissolute and ill-disciplined. In juxtaposition, Prospero casts himself as "princely" and stable ("trunk"), once again affirming his perspective on his brother's ill nature.
- "Verdure" continues the use of plant imagery; its literal meaning is vegetation, and here it figuratively depicts the freshness and vigour that once characterised Prospero's reign as Duke of Milan.

**Use in essays on…** Power; Betrayal; Relationships; Vengeance and Revenge.

**Act One Scene Two:**
**CALIBAN:** "This island's mine by Sycorax, my mother, / Which thou takest from me."

**Interpretation:** Caliban's opening lines present him as a traditional antagonist, yet also hint at the true horrors and consequences of colonisation.

**Techniques:** Tone; Language.

**Analysis:**
- In colonial terms, Caliban is entrapped mentally and physically; even his combative stance reinforces inevitable submission to his master. "This island's mine" presents an enigmatic, at times contradictory role. We are saddened by his submissive state; it is notable it takes several lines of dialogue for Caliban to state his claim.
- The audience are often conflicted, simultaneously disgusted by and endeared to his character; the tender tone of "my mother" humanises Caliban, and "tak'st from me" emphasises his loss, whilst the logic and legal understanding displayed in "mine, by Sycorax, my mother", reveals his intellect.
- One may argue Caliban is symbolic of the play as a whole; both funny and filled with pathos, victim and aggressor, he is a fusion of different theatrical ideas and rules, much like the tragicomedy of *The Tempest*.

**Use in essays on...** Power; Betrayal; Relationships; Colonisation.

**Act One Scene Two:**
**CALIBAN:** "O ho, O ho! Would 't had been done! / Thou didst prevent me. I had peopled else / This isle with Calibans."

**Interpretation:** Caliban displays no remorse for his attempted sexual assault of Miranda; the use of laughter here is one of the most chilling aspects of Caliban's character.

**Techniques:** Exclamation; Repetition; Tone.

**Analysis:**
- Repetition of "O ho!" heightens the nefarious nature of this moment, yet laughter adds a tone of stage musicality, sounding somewhat infantile in his response. The audience may interpret this as indicating Caliban's almost childlike state, his lack of development perhaps due to the intensity of Prospero's rule.
- The informal "thou" unearths the contradictory nature of Caliban's relationship with his oppressors (Prospero and Miranda); "thou" hints at his resentment, as well as his desire to rebel against their rule.
- Caliban's desire to "peopled else this isle with Calibans" depicts indignation. Yet, from a Darwinian perspective his desire to reproduce conveys a wish for survival or, perhaps, the audience may be aware of the isolation Caliban is linked to; both "peopled" and "Calibans" suggest a need for company.

**Use in essays on…** Power; Relationships; Vengeance and Revenge; Colonisation.

**Act Two Scene One:**
   **ALONSO:** "Why, how now? Ho, awake! Why are you drawn? / Wherefore this ghastly looking?"

**Interpretation:** After the usurpation of Prospero to the island, the audience are again presented with the fragility of authority against individual ambition and desire for power.

**Techniques:** Questioning; Dramatic Irony.

**Analysis:**

- "Drawn" could be read in two ways. In a literal sense, Sebastian has "drawn" his weapon ready to strike; however, "drawn" could be representative of Sebastian being "drawn" emotionally to power and status.
- "Ghastly" serves as a comment on Sebastian's appearance. Yet, when considering its etymology ('ghast', meaning 'to terrify'), it could be argued Shakespeare is presenting the notion of regicide, even in this brief moment, as terrifying, as well as the terrifying evils power and hubris lead many to commit.
- Another interpretation of "ghastly" is related to 'ghosts', perhaps a subtle presentation of the cyclical nature of betrayal in the play; while Antonio is liberated by the past, Prospero and perhaps Sebastian seem haunted by past events.

**Use in essays on…** Violence; Vengeance and Revenge; Betrayal.

**Act Two Scene Two:**
> **CALIBAN:** "Sometime am I/All wound with adders, who with cloven tongues/Do hiss me into madness."

**Interpretation:** Caliban's first soliloquy allows the audience to delve further into his psyche. If his first scene with Prospero casts him as the villainous antagonist, this moment allows us to see the more vulnerable side of Caliban.

**Techniques:** Soliloquy; Imagery; Sibilance.

**Analysis:**
- Caliban reveals the brutality he endures from Prospero. "Adders" alludes to the serpent in Genesis, depicting Prospero's magic as darker and less sanitised than before. Another interpretation, from Greek Mythology, is Caliban as a Medusa figure, slowly driven to "madness" for his sins. Like Medusa, he is an antihero, equally repugnant and endearing.
- The sibilant "hiss me into madness" emphasises the sinister nature of Prospero's torture; "wound" presents Caliban's physical pain and "madness" his mental suffering. The audience may question if the severity of Prospero's actions is accurately portrayed here, or a figment of Caliban's imagination.

**Use in essays in...** Power; Vengeance and Revenge; Colonisation.

### Act Two Scene Two:
> **STEPHANO: "Come on your ways. Open your mouth. Here is that which will give language to you, cat."**

**Interpretation:** Shakespeare presents the irony of supposedly sophisticated Europeans controlling the original inhabitants of the island; juvenile and drunken, their intellect is clearly lacking.

**Techniques:** Imperative; Language; Imagery.

**Analysis:**
- Alcohol misuse as base humour is associated with lower status characters of Shakespearean comedy; parallels with colonial masters who used alcohol to placate and oppress their subjects makes this scene uncomfortable for modern audiences.
- We are also discomforted by the parallels in the language used by Stephano and Prospero; imperatives such as "come" and "open" present a painful similarity and an awareness of their supposed superiority.
- The animalistic imagery of "cat" presents the dehumanisation Caliban continues to experience; it is ironic Stephano claims this "will give language to you" when Caliban is one of the most articulate inhabitants on the island.

**Use in essays on…** Power; Violence; Colonisation.

**Act Two Scene Two:**
   **TRINCULO: "But that the poor monster's in drink. An abominable monster!"**

**Interpretation:** In Naples, Stephano and Trinculo are lowly servants; however, on the island societal rules are upended and Trinculo finds himself assuming the role of a stately gentlemen, allowing Shakespeare to reveal the corruptive nature of power.

**Techniques:** Repetition; Language.

**Analysis:**

- Once again, the comedy conveys the darkness of the colonist mindset; the repetition of "monster" again unearths the colonialist perspective that anyone who does not fit the mould of Eurocentricity is abnormal.
- Repetition of "monster" emphasises and hones this cruelty. However, there is also an element of irony here; the truly "abominable" behaviour comes from Trinculo and Stephano, and they are the ones consumed with power and avarice.
- Caliban is once again placed at the bottom of a hierarchy, belittled as a "poor" monster. Despite being significantly more intelligent than Stephano and Trinculo, the audience glean a rather opportunistic element in the chastising of Caliban, designed to present the manipulative, selfish nature of many men on the island.

**Use in essays on…** Power; Violence; Colonisation.

**Act Two Scene Two:**
> **CALIBAN:** "Ban, 'ban, Ca-Caliban / Has a new master: get a new man. / Freedom, high-day! High-day, freedom! Freedom / high-day, freedom!"

**Interpretation:** Through the introduction of the lower status characters, Trinculo and Stephano, and the addition of their brash and base humour, the underlying commentary on class, race and colonisation reveals a serious element to the comic scene.

**Techniques:** Song; Repetition.

**Analysis:**
- This is a joyful song; the buoyant nature of "Ban, 'ban, Ca-Caliban", positive connotations of "high-day" and repetition of "freedom", along with the joyous, infantile tone, presents the audience with Caliban's possible hope for the future.
- However, the song reveals Caliban's naïve state of mind; despite a desire to serve a master that treats him with some semblance of respect, audiences are presented with the repetitive nature of colonisation. Although "new", he still has a "master".
- His joy is emotive as the audience observes the cyclical nature of oppression. Caliban sees hope through Stephano and Trinculo, two lower status characters, who only hold power as a result of their European heritage.

**Use in essays on…** Power; Relationships; Colonisation; Vengeance and Revenge; Class.

**Act Three Scene One:**
 **PROSPERO:** (Aside) "Poor worm, thou art infected! / This visitation shows it."

**Interpretation:** During Miranda and Ferdinand's romance, it could be argued Prospero's presence is a reflection on patriarchy; his status is always felt. We also see his manipulative nature - he refuses to abandon his power, even in Miranda's relationship.

**Techniques:** Staging; Imagery.

**Analysis:**
- Prospero's aside creates a tone of secrecy, with his secretive nature conveying a desire for supremacy; it also presents a somewhat cynical element to this love story. Is this more of a political marriage? Is it another way for Prospero to restore his power? Has their relationship been orchestrated as part of his plan?
- "Worm" and "infected" portray a rather pessimistic perspective on love, with "infected" presenting it as a disease. However, the audience could be witnessing the vulnerability that both father and daughter feel during this moment of change.
- Supernatural associations of "visitation" elevate Prospero's power, presenting him as spirit-like and, much like Ariel, allows him to maintain control over the action.

**Use in essays on…** Power; The Supernatural; Relationships; Gender.

**Act Three Scene Two:**
**STEPHANO: "Drink, servant-monster, when I bid thee. / Thy eyes are almost set in thy head."**

**Interpretation:** Stephano, Caliban's new master, exhibits similar qualities to Prospero. The epithet of "monster" has an underlying discomfort for the modern audience, with the explicit and implicit racism in calling a 'native' character a "monster".

**Techniques:** Imperative; Language.

**Analysis:**
- There is a sense of pathos in this scene. Whilst comic, the truth of colonisation is painfully presented; the cruelty of Stephano and Trinculo's treatment of Caliban makes the audience question the nature of the comedy.
- Did this scene work as comedy for a Jacobean audience? Does the awareness of colonisation from a modern audience prohibit them for enjoying the comedy?
- "Servant-monster" presents the duality of this insult; Caliban's life has been filled with servitude ("servant") due to his apparent differences ("monster"). The controlling "I bid thee" mimics the bondage Caliban suffered under Prospero, and "eyes are almost set in thy head" depicts Caliban losing control.

**Use in essays on…** Power; Relationships; Colonisation; Class.

**Act Three Scene Two:**
**CALIBAN:** "Batter his skull, or paunch him with a stake, / Or cut his wezand with thy knife."

**Interpretation:** Whilst the audience may view Caliban's murderous plan as presenting his antagonistic qualities, the importance of understanding Caliban as a more nuanced character makes this outburst more revealing in terms of his motivations.

**Techniques:** Language; Imagery.

**Analysis:**

- The harsh consonant filled sounds of the verbs "paunch", "cut", and the violent 't' and 'b' in "batter", convey the intensity of Caliban's hatred for Prospero.
- However, the notion Caliban is simply an aggressive brute is dispelled in the detailed manner in which he outlines his desires; as well as his sophisticated vocabulary, this presents Caliban as far more intelligent than first thought.
- "Wezand" (throat) could be literal; Caliban wants to slit Prospero's throat. Yet, a metaphorical interpretation could be Caliban wanting to both literally and figuratively remove Prospero's voice; in a similar way to Prospero diluting Caliban's cultural heritage, Caliban wants to eradicate the voice that has tortured him.

**Use in essays on…** Violence; Relationships; Vengeance and Revenge; Colonisation.

**Act Three Scene Two:**
**CALIBAN: "Be not afeard. The isle is full of noises, / Sounds and sweet airs that give delight and hurt not."**

**Interpretation:** After Ariel begins to torture them, Caliban attempts to soothe a terrified Stephano and Trinculo; his eloquence, appreciation of beauty and understanding of the island's joys present Caliban in a different light to the European perspectives of him.

**Techniques:** Sibilance; Imagery.

**Analysis:**
- Caliban's sensitive, cerebral side is once again revealed; the use of sibilance conveys a softer presentation, almost serenading Stephano and Trinculo, and the gentle sounds create a lyrical, lullaby quality. Is this possibly Caliban taking his rightful position as the ruler?
- We also see the juxtaposition between Caliban's perspective of the island, viewing it as "sweet" and a "delight", with the "cell" Prospero considers it.
- The magical nature of the "isle" is also presented in this moment. Rather than the frightening images the audience have been inundated with, the island is presented as mercurial and sensually enticing ("noises, sounds and sweet airs").

**Use in essays on…** Power; The Supernatural; Relationships.

**Act Three Scene Three:**
**ARIEL:** "But remember - / For that's my business to you - that you three / From Milan did supplant good Prospero."

**Interpretation:** Shakespeare uses Ariel to reveal an emphatic message about the importance of legitimacy amongst rulers, and of the evil of usurpation.

**Techniques:** Direct Address; Imperative; Dramatic Irony.

**Analysis:**

- The formal "business" and "supplant" reinforce the significant consequences of the actions of "you three". Whilst there is a focus on the human aspect of Prospero's revenge, there is legitimate "business" in his quest to restore order.
- Ariel's relationship with Prospero is open to interpretation, but "good Prospero" conveys a sincere and genuine tone, reinforcing Prospero's benevolent side.
- The direct address and imperative "But remember" reinforces the complex hierarchy on the island. Ariel holds power over a European king at this point, ordering him to "remember" his previous behaviour.
- There is dramatic irony in Ariel's speech; to "supplant good Prospero" is wrong, yet the audience is aware Prospero supplanted the island's original inhabitants.

**Use in essays on…** The Supernatural; Betrayal; Vengeance and Revenge.

**Act Four Scene One:**
**PROSPERO:** "Then, as my gift and thine own acquisition / Worthily purchased take my daughter."

**Interpretation:** On the surface, Prospero concedes his power, giving in to the marriage between his daughter and Ferdinand; however, Shakespeare reveals the power structures and politics at play in this marriage.

**Techniques:** Imagery; Language; Semantic Field.

**Analysis:**
- Prospero presents Miranda as a "gift", and similar to "cherub" in Act One Scene Two, in both moments we see the love he has for Miranda, yet it also presents the patriarchal ideals Prospero upholds – Miranda is objectified, a prize to be won.
- The semantic field of economic transaction permeates Prospero's statement. Ferdinand has "purchased" Miranda as something that forms an "acquisition".
- Contextually, a modern audience must be aware of a young woman being considered the property of her father before being acquired by her husband, something for him to "take". The transactional nature of marriage somewhat undermines the romantic moments we have seen between the young lovers.

**Use in essays on…** Power; Gender; Relationships.

**Act Four Scene One:**
> PROSPERO: "I had forgot that foul conspiracy/Of the beast Caliban and his confederates."

**Interpretation:** As varying narratives begin to conclude, Prospero remembers the sub-plot of revenge involving Caliban, revealing the motivating factors behind his behaviour.

**Techniques:** Imagery; Tone

**Analysis:**
- "Foul" once again establishes the scorn and malice Prospero has for Caliban; the fricative 'f' further establishes the venomous nature of Prospero's attack. The tempestuous, ferocious language of "foul" and "beast" characterise not only their relationship, but the emotionally charged style of the play as a whole.
- The animalistic imagery of "beast" once again underlines the dehumanisation of Caliban, portraying him as almost diabolic.
- "Confederates" (meaning accomplice), describes the bumbling fools that are Trinculo and Stephano, suggesting they are complicit in something nefarious. Prospero is again casting himself as a hero and Caliban as villain; it is important to consider who we as an audience consider the hero and villain of the play.

**Use in essays on…** Power; Vengeance and Revenge.

### Act Four Scene One:
### ARIEL: "I told you, sir, they were red-hot with drinking; / So full of valour that they smote the air."

**Interpretation:** Ariel's mocking, sarcastic tone towards the rebels is multi-faceted – does Ariel feel genuine anger towards them and true loyalty towards Prospero, or is this an opportunity for him to further his case for release from servitude?

**Techniques:** Imagery; Language.

**Analysis:**

- There is some unreliability in Ariel's perspective of the scene; Ariel has an obvious bias towards Prospero, be it genuine loyalty to him, or a desire to gain his freedom.
- The "red-hot" image is highly evocative; whilst depicting enjoyment of drink, it also paints a far more nefarious image. Caliban, often associated with demonic attitudes through his link to Sycorax, is also described as "red hot", with the diabolical imagery clear here.
- "Smote" has a slightly supernatural tone, almost in conflict with the natural elements, perhaps implying their desire to overthrow Prospero should be considered an unnatural deed.

**Use in essays on…** Power; Relationships; Violence.

**Act Four Scene One:**
   **CALIBAN:** "Thine own forever, and I, thy Caliban, / For aye thy foot-licker."

**Interpretation:** Caliban pledges servitude to Stephano, but his motivation is unclear. Is Caliban presented as subservient, or as a manipulator using Stephano for his own needs?

**Techniques:** Language; Imagery.

**Analysis:**
- On a superficial level this further reinforces the role of servant Caliban has been socialised to adopt; the imagery of "foot-licker" adds pathos and presents Caliban as a victim of colonisation, perhaps in contrast to Ariel's supposed agency.
- However, "Thine" and "thy" present a conniving, intelligent element to Caliban. "Thine" and "thy" pronouns are informal, possibly suggesting a sense of equality between himself and Stephano. The audience can question who is the true leader; is Caliban more of an orchestrator than a faithful servant? This instantly changes the audience's perception of him; we realise his intelligence, as well as his devious nature, and much like Ariel he is manipulating the situation to his own ends.
- However, many in the audience may applaud him for this rather than condemn; Caliban is more deserving of the land than they are.

**Use in essays on…** Power; Class; Colonisation.

**Act Four Scene One:**
> **PROSPERO:** "Fury, Fury! There, Tyrant, there! Hark! Hark!"

**Interpretation:** Whilst Ariel's language towards Stephano, Trinculo and Caliban is full of moral judgement, Prospero's language and actions are vicious, brutal and vengeful.

**Techniques:** Exclamation; Repetition; Tone.

**Analysis:**

- The "f" and "t" sounds here are harsh and allow Prospero's "fury" to be emphasised; the repetition of "fury" in addition to the fricative sounds creates a truly unpleasant tone. Prospero's relationship with Caliban is antagonistic and we often see this in the belligerent nature of their speech.
- Is this "fury" simply towards Caliban, or is there some inherent hatred towards himself? Is there any element of "fury" for his failures as a leader?
- Additionally, Prospero characterising Caliban as "tyrant" is rather hypocritical, with Prospero's behaviour towards Caliban and Ariel certainly somewhat tyrannical. In many ways, their tyranny parallels each other; both are victims of usurpation. They both desire power, however Caliban's lack of influence and societal status means he will always be relegated to a position of subservience.

**Use in essays on…** Violence; Relationships; Power; Colonisation.

**Act Five Scene One:**
**MIRANDA: "Sweet lord, you play me false."**
**FERDINAND: "No, my dearest love, / I would not for the world."**

**Interpretation:** Prospero reveals the happy couple to the rest of the inhabitants of the island; playing chess, Shakespeare presents them as pawns in Prospero's own game.

**Techniques:** Imagery; Tone.

**Analysis:**
- This reveal allows the comic ending of the play to be reaffirmed, with their partnership and impending marriage conforming to traits of the comedic genre.
- Chess, often used in literature to symbolise love and war, could symbolise the restoration of Prospero's kingdom, a key part of his plan to regain power; in many ways Miranda and Ferdinand's relationship is his final move for success.
- Miranda calls Ferdinand "sweet lord", an indication of her devotion to him, juxtaposed by her assertion he has played her "false", symbolic of the nature of fallacy in the play as a whole. The island serves as a mirage of society, reflecting and distorting it, but "sweet" and "dearest love" imply we are meant to appreciate this marriage as romantic as well as political.

**Use in essays on…** Power; Relationships; Gender.

**Act Five Scene One:**
**MIRANDA: "How beauteous mankind is! O, brave new world / That has such people in't!"**

**Interpretation:** Miranda instinctively sees "beauteous mankind"; Shakespeare presents her naive view in contrast to the audience's knowledge of who "such people" truly are.

**Techniques:** Exclamation; Language.

**Analysis:**
- The emotive "O" signifies the overwhelming response Miranda has in this moment. Her innocence and optimism are presented; largely isolated from the evils of society, she revels in her wonder at "how beauteous mankind is".
- What is this "brave new world"? There are allusions to the "new world" of America as coined by explorers of the Elizabethan and Jacobean era, yet for Miranda this is inverted; the "new world" she is about to enter is densely populated and less innocent, and ironically very few of these "people" are "brave".
- The promise of "new" ends this rather contradictory play in an overwhelmingly positive manner. This is in many ways not an ending, but rather a beginning for most of the characters, presuming the lessons of the play have been learnt.

**Use in essays on…** Power; Relationships; Gender.

**Act Five Scene One:**
**GONZALO:** "Look down, you god, /And on this couple drop a blessed crown!/ For it is you that have chalk'd forth the way / Which brought us hither."

**Interpretation:** Gonzalo's words present a positive, secure future, one led by "god" overseeing a rightful "couple" who are "blessed" moving along a predetermined "way".

**Techniques:** Imagery.

**Analysis:**
- Gonzalo's imagery highlights the restoration of legitimacy and order to the world. "Couple" implies unity; "crown" emphasises the return to legitimate leadership in Italy; and "blessed" confirms a return to a political order ordained by God.
- "You god" is open to interpretation; in some productions it is "you gods". Does "god" refer to a Christian god, with religion triumphing over the supernatural, or does "gods" legitimise Prospero's relationship with pagan gods? Is god's blessing reinstating the Great Chain of Being? Or is Gonzalo calling Prospero "god", deifying him and elevating his greatness – after all, Prospero is the one who "chalk'd forth the way/Which brough us hither."
- "Chalk'd forth" and "brought us" present images of control and manipulation, but without the darker insinuations of earlier in the play; instead, they are protective.

**Use in essays on…** Power; The Supernatural.

**Act Five Scene One:**

**SEBASTIAN: "Will money buy 'em?"**
**ANTONIO: "Very like. One of them/Is a plain fish, and no doubt marketable."**

**Interpretation:** For all the contrition, humility and new-found understanding displayed by Gonzalo and Alonso, the darker elements of human greed, manipulation and control are still present at the end of the play.

**Techniques:** Imagery; Semantic Field.

**Analysis:**
- Amongst the lessons learnt by many members of the court, Shakespeare presents a lingering element of corrupt European behaviour; the behaviour of Antonio and Sebastian continues to be selfish and driven by their own ambitions.
- A semantic field of business reminds the audience that Prospero will not be returning to the utopia Gonzalo depicted – "money", "buy'em" and "marketable" highlight that Milan is still driven by greed and ambition in a world that sees people as something to trade and profit from.
- Ideas of usurpation have not been defeated by the end of the play – the powerful figure of Antonio sees the weaker "plain fish" (Caliban) and instantly asserts ownership over him, much like Prospero and Stephano before him.

**Use in essays on…** Colonisation; Power; Class.

**Epilogue:**
**PROSPERO:** "Now I want / Spirits to enforce, art to enchant, / And my ending is despair, / Unless I be relieved by prayer."

**Interpretation:** Prospero's final speech and the last words of the play convey his desire for the island to be restored to "spirits", "art" and enchantment, but also highlight the "despair" his behaviour may have caused.

**Techniques:** Tone; Direct Address.

**Analysis:**
- Prospero's need to be "relieved by prayer" links to the overt religiosity of the intended audience. Prospero as a 'sorcerer' or 'magician' is presented in a rather secular manner, closer to the notion of alchemy than magic; he repeatedly refers to "art", not magic, which would be seen as sacrilegious and somewhat demonic.
- There is a vulnerability to Prospero here; "I want" and "unless" both imply he is not in full control of his destiny, and "my ending is despair" seems to be admittance of his own wrongdoings throughout the play.
- Is Prospero saddened by his past transgressions? Is the finality in this speech genuine? Or do the audience and other characters need some admittance of Prospero's wrongdoing to forgive him? Either of these interpretations are valid.

**Use in essays on…** Relationships; Power; The Supernatural.

## Major Themes

| | | |
|---|---|---|
| Violence | Power | Class |
| Colonisation | Vengeance and Revenge | Relationships |
| Betrayal | The Supernatural | Gender |

## Major Characters

| | | |
|---|---|---|
| Prospero | Miranda | Caliban |
| Ariel | Alonso | Ferdinand |
| Stephano | Trinculo | Antonio |
| Sebastian | | Gonzalo |

## How to revise effectively.

One mistake people often make is to try to revise EVERYTHING!

This is clearly not possible.

Instead, once you know and understand the plot, a great idea is to pick three or four major themes, and three or four major characters, and revise these in great detail.

If, for example, you revised Miranda and Power, you will also have covered a huge amount of material to use in questions about Gender, Relationships or Ferdinand.

Or, if you revised Prospero and Colonisation, you would certainly have plenty of material if a question on Betrayal, Violence or Caliban was set.

Use the following framework as a basis for setting *any* of your own revision questions – simply swap the theme or character to create a new essay title!

**How does Shakespeare portray the theme of _____ in *The Tempest*?**

**How does the character of _____ develop as the play progresses?**

## A sample essay paragraph (top level), using ideas directly from The Quotation Bank (page 16).

### *How does Shakespeare present Caliban throughout the play?*

Through the introduction of the lower status characters, Trinculo and Stephano, and the addition of their brash and base humour, Shakespeare utilises the character of Caliban to explore the underlying commentary on class, race and colonisation and to reveal a serious element to the comic scene. Caliban delivers a joyful song; the buoyant nature of "Ban, 'ban, Ca-Caliban", positive connotations of "high-day" and repetition of "freedom", along with the joyous, infantile tone, presents the audience with Caliban's possible hope for the future. However, the song reveals Caliban's naïve state of mind; despite a desire to serve a master that treats him with some semblance of respect, audiences are presented with the repetitive nature of colonisation; although "new", he still has a "master". His joy is emotive as the audience observes the cyclical nature of oppression. Caliban sees hope through Stephano and Trinculo, two lower status characters, who only hold power as a result of their European heritage.

## Potential Essay Questions
## What is the significance of the supernatural in *The Tempest*?

**Topic Sentence 1:** Shakespeare presents a complex relationship between Prospero and the supernatural to reinforce the audience's fear of the supernatural world.

**Use:** Pages 8 and 31.

**Topic Sentence 2:** The audience's fear is reinforced by Shakespeare's presentation of the dark, threatening elements of the supernatural.

**Use:** Pages 12 and 13.

**Topic Sentence 3:** The supernatural is further presented as dominant over human concerns.

**Use:** Pages 21 and 24.

**Topic Sentence 4:** However, Shakespeare also presents a pure, religious element to the supernatural.

**Use:** Pages 20 and 29.

# How is Caliban portrayed in *The Tempest*?

**Topic Sentence 1:** Shakespeare presents Caliban as a stereotypical monster to examine the audience's views of the 'other'.

**Use:** Pages 11 and 15.

**Topic Sentence 2:** However, Shakespeare also presents Caliban as a victim of supposed European superiority and power.

**Use:** Pages 18 and 25.

**Topic Sentence 3:** Shakespeare presents Caliban in a sympathetic light to explore the consequences of the harsh treatment he suffers.

**Use:** Pages 13 and 23.

**Topic Sentence 4:** Finally, Shakespeare depicts Caliban as an intelligent, sophisticated character to challenge the audience's prejudices.

**Use:** Pages 10 and 20.

## How are relationships presented in *The Tempest*?

**Topic Sentence 1:** For much of the play, Shakespeare explores the corrupt nature of relationships to challenge the hierarchy of contemporary society.

**Use:** Pages 9, 16 and 26.

**Topic Sentence 2:** Shakespeare presents the power and hierarchy within these relationships to examine ideas around human control.

**Use:** Pages 7, 12 and 30.

**Topic Sentence 3:** However, many of the relationships portray the purity and beauty that can be found in human relationships.

**Use:** Pages 22, 27 and 28.

**Topic Sentence 4:** Perhaps the most powerful relationship within the play is the father/daughter one, which allows Shakespeare to explore Prospero's motivations.

**Use:** Pages 8 and 17.

## How does Prospero develop throughout the play?

**Topic Sentence 1:** Shakespeare presents Prospero as a victim of betrayal and usurpation to explore ideas relating to legitimacy and power.

**Use:** Pages 9, 21 and 23.

**Topic Sentence 2:** However, Shakespeare also presents Prospero as a tyrant and abusive leader to further examine these ideas of legitimacy and hierarchy.

**Use:** Pages 10 and 13.

**Topic Sentence 3:** The action of the play is driven by Shakespeare's presentation of Prospero as a restorer, seeking to secure his daughter's birthright.

**Use:** Pages 8 and 22.

**Topic Sentence 4:** It is perhaps this role as a father that Shakespeare presents as the prime motivation for Prospero's actions throughout the play.

**Use:** Pages 17 and 22.

## Suggested Revision Activities

**Major character and themes** – Take any of the major characters and themes (see page 32 for a list) and group together quotations in sets of 2 or 3 to answer the following question: "How does the theme/character develop as the play goes on?"

You should try to get 4 sets of quotations, giving you 8-12 overall.

**A great cover and repeat exercise** – Cover the whole page, apart from the quotation at the top. Can you now fill in the four sections in your exercise book without looking – Interpretations, Techniques, Analysis, Use in essays on…?

This also works really well as **a revision activity with a friend** – cover the whole card, apart from the quotation at the top. If you read out the quotation, can they tell you the four sections without looking – Interpretations, Techniques, Analysis, Use in essays on…?

"The Development Game" – Pick any quotation at random from The Quotation Bank and use it to create an essay question, and then create a focused topic sentence to start the essay. Next, find another appropriate quotation to develop your idea even further.

"The Contrast Game" – Follow the same rules as The Development Game, but instead of finding a quotation to support your idea, find a quotation that can be used to start a counter-argument.

Your very own Quotation Bank! Using the same headings and format as The Quotation Bank, find 10 more quotations from throughout the text (select them from many different sections of the text to help develop whole text knowledge) and create your own revision cards.

Essay writing – They aren't always fun, but writing essays is great revision. Choose a practice question and then try taking three quotations and writing out a perfect paragraph, making sure you add connectives, technical vocabulary and sophisticated language.

## Glossary

**Alliteration** – Repetition of the same consonant or sound at the beginning of a number of words in a sentence: Sebastian's language has a fiery, volatile quality to it, reinforced by the violent associations of "bawling" and the harsh, aggressive alliteration of the 'b' sound in "bawling, blasphemous".

**Dramatic Irony** – When the audience knows something the characters don't: there is dramatic irony in Ariel's speech; to "supplant good Prospero" is wrong, yet the audience is aware Prospero supplanted the island's original inhabitants.

**Exclamation** – A word or phrase that expresses sudden emotion: the emotive "O" signifies the overwhelming response Miranda has in this moment.

**Imagery** – Figurative language that appeals to the senses of the audience: the use of horticultural imagery helps represent the growth of resentment, as well as the insidious way his brother stole power from him.

**Imperative** – A sentence that gives a command or an order: we are also discomforted by the parallels in the language used by Stephano and Prospero; imperatives such as "come" and "open" present a painful similarity and an awareness of their supposed superiority.

**Juxtaposition** – Two ideas, images or words placed next to each other to create a contrasting effect: we see the juxtaposition between Caliban's perspective of the island, viewing it as "sweet" and a "delight", with the "cell" Prospero considers it.

**Language** – The vocabulary chosen to create effect.

**Metaphor** – A word or phrase used to describe something else so that the first idea takes on the associations of the second: "Wezand" (throat) could be literal; Caliban wants to slit Prospero's throat, but a metaphorical interpretation could be Caliban wanting to both literally and figuratively remove Prospero's voice.

**Repetition** – When a word, phrase or idea is repeated to reinforce it: the repetition of "monster" again unearths the colonialist perspective that anyone who does not fit the mould of Eurocentricity is abnormal.

**Semantic Field** – A group of words used together from the same topic area: a semantic field of economic transaction permeates Prospero's statement. Ferdinand has "purchased" Miranda as something that forms an "acquisition".

**Sibilance** – A variation on alliteration, usually of the 's' sound, that creates a hissing sound: the sibilant "hiss me into madness" emphasises the sinister nature of Prospero's torture.

**Soliloquy** – A speech when a character talks to themselves: Caliban's first soliloquy allows the audience to delve further into his psyche.

**Tone** – The way the writer has ordered the words in a sentence to create a certain effect: the audience are often conflicted, simultaneously disgusted by and endeared to Caliban's character; the tender tone of "my mother" humanises Caliban, and "tak'st from me" emphasises his loss.

**Staging** – Directions given to the director or actor to aid interpretation: Prospero's aside creates a tone of secrecy, with his secretive nature conveying a desire for supremacy; it also presents a somewhat cynical element to this love story.